ICEHC

Tim Buxbaum

SHIRE PUBLICATIONS

Published in Great Britain in 2014 by Shire Publications Ltd, PO Box 883, Oxford, OX1 9PL, UK.

PO Box 3985, New York, NY 10185-3985, USA.

E-mail: shire@shirebooks.co.uk www.shirebooks.co.uk

A CIP catalogue record for this book is available from the British Library.

Shire Library no. 769. ISBN-13: 978 0 74781 300 2

Tim Buxbaum has asserted his right under the Copyright, Designs and Patents Act, 1988, to be identified as the author of this book.

Designed by Tony Trucott Designs, Sussex, UK and typeset in Perpetua and Gill Sans.

Printed in China through Worldprint Ltd.

14 15 16 17 18   10 9 8 7 6 5 4 3 2 1

COVER IMAGE
Cover design by Peter Ashley and photography of icehouse at Compton Verney in Warwickshire by Philip Wilkinson; back cover detail: early nineteenth-century dessert.

TITLE PAGE IMAGE
An architectural 'pattern-book' icehouse design from the 1790s has been attributed to the neoclassical architect John Soane.

CONTENTS PAGE IMAGE
William Kent's banqueting house at Euston Hall, built directly above the earlier conical icewell, yet seemingly retaining access to it. A more functional icehouse was added later, probably in the nineteenth century, much closer to the hall.

ACKNOWLEDGEMENTS
would like to thank the many people who have allowed me to visit icehouses on their land, and consult their archives. The illustrations are acknowledged as follows:

Alexandre de Vendeuvre, page 46 bottom; Archivos Municipales de Somontano de Barbastro, Huesca, Spain, page 4 left; Ballina Hotel, Ireland, page 49 bottom; Beyond My Ken WM, Wikicommon, page 47 bottom; British Library, pages 10 and 34 bottom; Collection of the Museum of London WM, page 9 top; Ecelan WM, Wikicommon, page 45; Enrique Iniguez Rodriguez WM, Wikicommon page 44; Hemming Jorgensen, pages 41, 42, 48; Illustrated London News, page 25; Jochen Jahnke at de.wikipedia, page 46 top; John Goom, architect, page 16; London Canal Museum (drawing by Brian Alldridge 1996), page 40; National Records of Scotland (RHP 13257/68, Alloa, Sep 1727), page 30; National Trust, pages 7, 28, 33 bottom; Soane Museum (Adam volume 37/11), page 32 top. All the other photographs and drawings are by the author.

WORDS FOR ICEHOUSE IN FOREIGN LANGUAGES

French: *glacière*

German: *Eiskeller*

Italian: *ghiacciaia, diaccer, giassera, giazera*

Spanish: *nevera, neverone, pozos de la nieve, elurzulo*

CONTENTS

Below:
Spanish *neveros*
(snow gatherers)
cut a layer of ice
from the chamber
and lift it by bucket
and pulley to
ground level, where
it is loaded into a
mule's panniers for
overnight transport
to market.

Below right:
At a similar
elevation to Ben
Nevis, the stone-
ribbed crown of
the huge Cava
Arquejada icehouse
probably supported
a roof covering, but
could have been a
symbolic open-
work marker in
the mountains; the
fragile finial is now
cradled in timber.

INTRODUCTION

Before refrigerators were invented, snow was brought down from mountaintops to cities in order to cool refreshing drinks. From ancient times it was carried from Mount Etna to Rome, from Mount Bursa to Istanbul, and from the Sierra Nevada to Granada in southern Spain, where the trade continued into the nineteenth century. Snow gatherers led their mules up the mountains on summer afternoons, filled their panniers by night and returned to the city before sunrise to sell through the heat of the day. In places where the supply of snow was less reliable, it was collected, compacted and sheltered in sufficient quantities to last throughout the year, or even several years. Most ancient civilisations did this, including the Egyptians, Greeks, Romans and Chinese; often it involved filling a pit with snow or ice, then covering it with branches and straw.

Who can say when the courtesy of cooled drinks arrived in Britain? Perhaps the Medieval Warm Period stimulated a demand for ice in summer, or maybe

the Little Ice Age, which followed, encouraged the storage of ice by generating larger quantities. The climate chilled noticeably through the fifteenth century, affecting the way people lived. Many cold winters were recorded between 1650 and 1850 (1708 was possibly Europe's coldest) and then temperatures rose. It is tempting to correlate the history of icehouses with climatic change, but that is simplistic; these buildings also track political stability, wealth and power. In Britain, substantial icehouses were symbols of luxury, and thus a low priority at times of unrest. Humbler structures are not recorded, and early techniques of ice storage may have been forgotten during such upheavals as the Dissolution of the Monasteries and the Civil War.

In Mediterranean Europe, stone structures were built before 1500 to store snow for palaces, abbeys, monasteries and castles, serving nobility, refreshing pilgrims, providing income and assisting the sick. Less permanent structures were also built. Snow became 'a monopoly that produces a revenue to the Pope', and from 1596 to 1855 taxes from the sale of snow in Mexico went to the King of Spain.

In medieval Britain, ice could have been collected from frozen fishponds, moats and millponds, and used to chill wine imported from Gascony from the fourteenth century. As the merchant John Frampton observed in 1580, ice is 'used in the courts of kings, princes, great men, lords and common people residing there'. Frampton's Elizabethan readers knew that chilled water was beneficial against hot humours and would improve a glass of wine. In hot weather, iced plums, apples, cherries and melons were particularly refreshing, as were cold meats. Of course, the ice had to be selected with care, lest it be corrupted by 'rotten plantes, naughtie trees … and dead babies'. Frampton's translation of his Spanish sourcebook mentions 'snow houses' in Flanders,

Hungary and Bohemia, but overlooks the huge snow pits of south-eastern Spain, perhaps dating from the fifteenth century and linked to southern Italy, Corsica and Sardinia by the Crown of Aragon. The old Spanish pits were so large that in 1762, following heavy snowfall, a thousand men and seven hundred horses were despatched to help fill them.

Two surviving early-nineteenth-century icehouses in Britain, at Burton Manor and Penrhyn Castle, suggest a family of early structures that do not seem to have been widely documented as ice stores. One is a tunnel, the other an oubliette. A subterranean tunnel icehouse was excavated from the bedrock at Burton Manor in 1805, creating two interlinked chambers that were filled through an opening at ground level, and accessed at each end by a flight of external steps. That arrangement gives credence to stories of other underground ice stores, for example among the five hundred caves dug out in the post-medieval period below Nottingham – especially those associated with taverns. It also brings to mind souterrains, and the ancient underground stairways, tunnels and vaults of important castles such as Pontefract, Conwy and St Andrews. St Andrews Castle in Fife, ruinous by 1656, had been one of the most important medieval residences in Scotland – an archbishop's palace in a city with international links; just the sort of place where chilled wines for banquets might be expected. It also has an oubliette or bottle dungeon, believed to date from the chilly fifteenth century, accessible only from a manhole-sized opening at the top, through which a man on a rope could descend to collect ice, or provisions could be lowered in baskets. In a warmer climate prisoners might have languished in such places, but perhaps their original function was for cold storage near kitchens and the great hall – as is clear in the ice tower of Penrhyn Castle, an 1830s recreation of a Norman castle. At Penrhyn, an external door at the base of the tower enabled ice to be loaded into the chamber below, but day-to-day use seems to have been by means of the man-sized opening through the floor of the room above, just like that of an oubliette. Something similar, on a smaller scale, survives at Bedwellty, Caerphilly, and also in Wales, perhaps preserving the traditions of the castle-building period, is the modest ice chamber at the base of the garden pavilion in Dunraven Park, in the Vale of Glamorgan, which provided refreshment for visitors.

Far left:
At the base of Penrhyn Castle's ice tower is a conical ice chamber 23 feet deep, accessible both from a low-level external door and this opening in the floor above it. The hole is protected by a wooden bung, operated by a pulley, through which basketfuls of ice or chilled provisions could be raised.

Left:
The icehouse chamber at Penrhyn Castle is protected by two doors at ground level. The lobby between them gives access to a curved passageway part way round the outside of the chamber, perhaps used in conjunction with the walled garden.

Uncertainties about the use of ice in medieval castles are illustrated in Viollet-le-Duc's *Dictionnaire Raisonné de l'Architecture Française* covering the period from the eleventh to the sixteenth centuries. Volume 6, published in 1863, under *Oubliettes* illustrates a chamber at the Bastille in Paris that Viollet-le-Duc concedes was probably an icehouse – and not the only one he had seen in a medieval French castle. Perhaps rising winter temperatures just after the medieval period rendered the older ice chambers in Britain swiftly redundant, or maybe they were aspirational and never really worked.

The earliest recorded purpose-built English snow well lined with brick dates from 1619, when James I had one dug at Greenwich to chill his wine. There seems to have been limited understanding of refrigeration, for it was with evident surprise in 1626 that the philosopher Francis Bacon recorded that a dead fowl packed in snow could be kept fresh. At the time of the Civil War in Britain, many people who might have built an icehouse escaped abroad, where they experienced these buildings first-hand. For example, the diarist John Evelyn travelled in France and Italy for three years from 1643 and in Padua drank wine cooled with snow and ice 'as the manner here is'. On his return he was a talented garden designer who knew about icehouses, typical of the sophisticated traveller familiar with their use abroad, who popularised the custom back home. With the restoration of the monarchy in 1660, there was a revival in architecture, the arts, garden design and in culinary skills. During his exile, Charles II had seen Versailles and now he wanted an English counterpart.

English icehouses of this period seem to have had limited success, presumably reflecting a lack of expertise, but circumstances encouraged perseverance. The winter of 1683–4 was particularly bitter, and annual frost fairs took place on the Thames, which froze solid for weeks at a time. When summer arrived, John Evelyn complained about the excessive heat, and he must have yearned for the cool drinks being enjoyed in the French and Spanish courts, while being fascinated by travellers' tales of icehouses in Persia. As the British gentry embarked on Grand Tours, they became increasingly familiar with icehouses in Europe. At the same time, there were innovations in building

construction, especially the use of brickwork, a good material with which to build an icehouse. It was not long before icehouses began to contribute to the enjoyment of the gardens of country houses across Britain, by providing refreshment and conferring prestige, by becoming architectural features and by serving the kitchen and walled garden. The fashion became widespread, and if an icehouse failed it brought embarrassment.

Away from the country estates, larger commercial icehouses were developed by confectioners, the fishing industry and shopkeepers. They appeared in the basements of town houses, supplied by horse and cart from central depots. Thus an international ice trade developed, transporting huge quantities of ice around the world until the early twentieth century. By then rising temperatures had cut the amount of natural ice available, which was increasingly at risk from pollution, and artificial refrigeration had been invented. Icehouses ceased to be used and were largely forgotten.

There has been a revival of interest in these structures because of the stories they tell. Many are tied to a technology and a way of life that are unrecognisable in the twenty-first century. Many were built at the peak of an enterprise, in a different climate, in a different economy. Their limited documentation adds an air of mystery and presents a challenge to researchers, whilst the chambers themselves are deeply atmospheric. Although inherently robust, they seem to have an ephemeral nature: some are still unrecognised in otherwise well-documented landscapes, awaiting rediscovery by future generations.

The Frozen Thames was painted in 1677 by Abraham Hondius, showing the dramatic extent of the ice. Old London Bridge is in the background; it probably acted as a dam, for the Thames did not freeze again after its demolition in 1814.

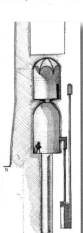

A sketch based on another of Viollet-le-Duc's drawings shows the base of the south-west tower of Pierrefonds Castle near Compiègne, a fortress rebuilt between 1393 and 1407. The vaulted upper chamber evidently provided access to a snow store below, from which cooled meltwater could be drawn off by bucket.

DESIGN AND APPEARANCE

O N COUNTRY ESTATES many icehouses were built in isolated positions, but they are also found near water features, beside walled gardens, within a ring of trees, under banqueting houses, and as part of larger buildings. Usually they would have been accessible by horse and cart, and today may be identified by a conical thatched roof, an exposed hemispherical brick vault or an artificial earth mound, with an entrance tunnel attached.

In the 1660s several 'snow wells' were dug in London – five for the royal household in gardens at St James's Palace and one for the Duchess of Cleveland. They were large brick 'flowerpots', tapering out from a low-level timber platform to a wider rim at ground level, then roofed in thatch on a timber frame and filled up with snow. By 1691 they were reportedly decayed, yet, in that year, an additional one was proposed by the architect Hawksmoor. The Duchess's snow well was rediscovered in 1956 and proved to be 13 feet deep, tapering out from a diameter of 7 feet 3 inches diameter at the base to 13 feet 5 inches at the top. In 1690 ownership of the structure had passed to the Duchess's son, the Duke of Grafton, who five years earlier had inherited Euston Hall, Suffolk, following its major reconstruction (1666–70) by the Earl of Arlington. At that time, Euston's grounds were being laid out to designs by John Evelyn. Euston's first icehouse dates from this period and takes the form of a great conical brick chamber sunk 26 feet into an elevated site – a significant development of the 'flowerpot' design. The cone is a scaled-down version of Evelyn's detailed description of 'the snow pits of Italy' quoted in the 1683 reprint of Robert Boyle's book *New Experiments Touching Cold*; it resembles an ice-cream cornet or old-fashioned sugar loaf, flaring out from the base and originally covered with a double thatched roof. The deep excavation required was challenging, but the setting out and construction of a brick cone was relatively straightforward, producing a form with inherent strength, and having much in common with the inverted brick cone 18 inches thick and 85 feet high eventually chosen to support the dome of

Opposite: Drawing of 'an Italian icehouse' similar to that described by John Evelyn, from *The Works of the Hon Robert Boyle*, Volume 2 (1744). The open-top conical chamber, with a supporting grating near the base, is insulated with a thatched roof, through which a small doorway provides access.

A wooden ladder disappears into the deep, cone-shaped brick chamber at Euston Hall, at the base of which the timber platform survives.

St Paul's Cathedral, raised in 1702 – a further project in which Evelyn had an interest. An icehouse cone like Euston's survives at the Governor's Palace at Williamsburg, Virginia, supposedly also designed by Wren and built from 1706. There are more recent interpretations of the conical shape, for example at Scotney Castle, Kent, but they tend to be smaller in scale, because of the cost of deep excavation. The conical form was effective: as the frozen mass within slowly melted and dropped, it remained intact, and the wide top gave a generous cool surface area.

Although the thatched timber roofs of these structures provided insulation, they were insecure and liable to catch fire from tapers used to illuminate the frosty depths. A step forward was the use of a brick dome built using timber formwork supported on the lip of the conical chamber, as was added on top of Euston's cone prior to the 1740s, when William Kent's banqueting house was built above it. That arrangement of a cone with a ledge or lip, at or above the highest level of the ice, providing support for a dome, is termed a 'cup and dome' design and it marks the progression to chambers with more rounded shapes, providing greater capacity with shallower excavation. The geometrical complexity of the most sophisticated examples required building skills that were not readily available in Britain in the seventeenth century, but at Castle Lyon (now Castle Huntly) near Dundee, at least the lower part of an almost egg-shaped brick-lined chamber was built between 1660 and 1690 by one of Charles II's courtiers. Sometimes builders demonstrated their inability to construct truly rounded shapes, like the 'two pyramids base to base' of the 1660s example at Tristernagh, or the eight-segmented brick base rising to an octagonal plan at Rufford Abbey.

The most impressive chambers were built in one operation, particularly during the eighteenth century, omitting an obvious lip and taking the shape of pears, milk bottles or demijohns, roofed with steep or shallow domes. The optimum shape was the most complex to build – an upended egg with the wider end as the base. Probably the bricklaying skills necessary to achieve the curves and vaults of such icehouses arrived from the Low Countries with the Glorious Revolution of William III and Mary II's accession to the British throne in 1689; the plot to achieve that was hatched in the Grove icehouse built at

Charborough in 1686. As well as brick, finely sculpted stone-lined chambers were also constructed, as at Whim House in the Scottish Borders. By the nineteenth century many icehouses reverted to simpler forms with vertical sides, showing a more targeted use of technology acquired through experience.

The icehouse that can still be seen at Hampton Court was proposed in 1690 and handed over in July 1693, with a 'floor' added in 1697. Boarding, flooring and roofing continued until 1700, as well as laying lead and encircling the structure with iron bands, as recommended by James Frontin, Yeoman of His Majesty's Ice Wells. Twelve encircling lime trees were not planted until 1702, when the original roof was thatched. The amount of time spent on this project reflected separate phases of construction, and a join is still visible from where the stepped brickwork of the original 'flowerpot' snow well was subsequently raised up into an impressively domed chamber with a great apex vent, around which was added a twelve-sided enclosure, carrying a substantial timber-framed roof. The voids between the inner and outer walls unexpectedly contain a small room with fireplace and chimney.

Huge handmade bricks separate the base of the chamber, which is 13 feet 3 inches high and 12 feet in diameter, from the bedrock at Castle Huntly. The icehouse was built 100 yards from the castle walls and close to a new freezing pond.

An unusually shallow brick-vaulted roof springs from a ledge at the top of the chamber of the icehouse at The Quarters, Alresford, Essex, which complements a chinoiserie fishing lodge from the 1770s.

The 18-foot-diameter egg-shaped chamber at Hampton Court icehouse rises from an earlier brick 'flowerpot' base to a large circular opening in the crown of the vault, providing ventilation. The entrance passage is 8 feet long and 4 feet wide.

Constructing an icehouse could be a complex operation and many different recommendations are recorded. For example, how big should the chamber be? They are rarely less than 6 feet in diameter and range between 8 feet and over 33 feet in height. One writer suggested that the right size would hold a hundred loads of ice, 'enough to supply a mansion for a year', but, as logistics improved, it was sometimes easier to manage a smaller chamber that could be regularly replenished from a natural source, or from a commercial distributor. The quality of ice and the care and frequency with which the store was used were significant. The chamber wall construction was important too, with much discussion of the relative merits of single- or double-skinned walls as thick as 2 feet, perhaps protected externally with a 1-foot thickness of puddled clay. Pedants distinguished between snow and

At Hampton Court a twelve-sided enclosure has been constructed around the perimeter of an earlier egg-shaped icehouse chamber largely built above ground, helping to insulate and buttress it, and support the substantial roof, which was originally thatched.

ice wells (built below ground), icehouses (largely built above) and ice towers, but most agreed that one large chamber was sufficient, with a secondary chamber in the more elaborate examples. An exception is at Petworth, where the large icehouse was rebuilt in 1784 as three separately accessed compartments beneath a dairy.

After about 1700 the roofs of most icehouse chambers were domed in close-jointed

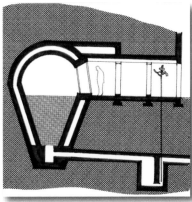

Left:
An icehouse design from Charles MacIntosh's *Book of the Garden* (1853), showing a range of sophisticated features including cavity wall construction, a shelved recess for storage outside the main chamber, and a pump for the extraction of chilled water from the sump.

brick or dressed stone; later domes were often flatter than earlier hemispherical domes. In December 1794 the icehouse at Taymouth Castle, Perthshire, was almost complete: 'It only requires doors, a covering of earth and the centres or moulding taken out.' Sometimes domes included air vents (more often in later structures), and quite often a central opening at the crown of the dome assisted loading, ventilation and occasionally extraction. Warm air and noxious gases could be produced by decaying

Below:
The chambers built for ice storage for the Duke of Argyll beneath Inveraray Castle, Argyll, 'would not answer', so a new, freestanding structure was built in four months in 1786.

insulation, so a sealed chamber risked overwhelming visitors and also increased the likelihood of condensation.

Normally the dome would be covered with a generous thickness of soil, or thatched for insulation. There was much discussion about the relative merits of these methods: an earth mound might be simpler and could support planting; a thatched structure was perhaps more decorative, yet more demanding to maintain. Despite that, examples survive in 'Capability' Brown landscapes at Compton Verney, Croome Park, Holkham and Heveningham Hall. One commentator suggested a 2-foot thickness of thatch finished in lime plaster below and slates or tiles above; others simply a thick waterproofing layer of tar. Often an early thatched roof simply rotted away, as on the twin domes at Studley Royal, exposing brickwork to the elements. Some ingenious operators achieved shade in other ways, by building their icehouse in the lee of a wall (Monk Bar, York), or under a bridge, either freestanding (Paxton House) or integrated (Mount Edgecumbe). In mainland Europe, several enthusiasts of the later eighteenth century deployed the most extreme design – the placing of an icehouse within a garden pyramid.

The icehouse would fail if the chamber retained moisture, either leaching in from the ground outside, from condensation, or from a build-up of meltwater, which had to be drained away. A timber platform supporting

The icehouse at Croome Park was repaired and re-thatched for insulation purposes, temporarily exposing the roof structure of rafters carried over the brick dome. Earlier structures would not have had a brick vault above the chamber.

the mass of ice was ideal, or a cartwheel laid convex side up. Underneath, there might be a sump – that at Powys Castle was 4 feet in diameter and 3 feet deep – or else a casting in iron, maybe with a grille in perforated zinc, connected to a drain using a gooseneck trap to exclude vermin and warm air. Regular cleaning of the drain avoided blockages, and at Tyntesfield a crawl passage was provided. Ideally, the drain discharged into a nearby stream or lake, but at Wynnstay House, Wrexham, the drain built in 1776 extended 123 yards because of site levels.

A few chambers were linked by a single lockable door directly to the world outside, but the majority were separated by a passage, typically around 10 feet long, 4 feet wide and high enough to stand up in, below a vaulted ceiling. The passage usually opened axially into the upper part of the chamber, its floor level close to the top of the ice; without the ice there is a hazardous drop. Many alternative designs for passages included changes of direction, secondary storage areas, recesses in the walls for tapers, candles or lanterns, and variations in level, necessitating flights of steps. Quite often, a short passage would have been extended on more than one occasion, presumably to try to improve insulation. The

longer or more convoluted the passage, the greater the likelihood that it was subdivided with as many as four internal doors, producing insulating 'strawsheds' to exclude warm air – using barley straw in rope-net bags, or canvas bags 'like immense cushions'. If the doors were edged in leather within substantial frames, they were effective, though time-consuming to operate. Perhaps in those cases there was benefit in sealing the passage and accessing the chamber only from above.

The emergence of the passage through a grassy mound is sometimes the only external evidence of an icehouse. There was much debate about the best orientation for the door, a little morning sun being preferred before the onset of shade. Many entrances were utilitarian – simple masonry surrounds with a secure door. More decorative results appeared in higher-status structures, for example Queen Victoria's icehouse at Osborne House,

Just outside York's city walls, and shaded by them and Monk Bar gate, this early-nineteenth-century brick icehouse is built into the slope of the ramparts. The chamber is just over 12 feet in diameter.

Paxton House, designed by John Adam and built in 1758–63, is reached by a bridge across the River Tweed. Sheltered under the bridge, the igloo-shaped icehouse has a finely vaulted stone roof and may have been used in conjunction with the estate salmon fishery.

17

Holkham Hall was built from 1734 by Thomas Coke following his return in 1718 from a six-year Grand Tour. The thatched icehouse may date from then, but it has been modified many times. The landscaped lake below retains a low stone wall, apparently to dam a freezing pond.

where the 1846 entrance was lengthened by 8 feet and refaced in 1853 to a design by Ludwig Gruner. It included many refinements: asphalt waterproofing; a 4-foot-square opening in the crown of the vault, ideal for delivering ice by the cartload into a large circular chamber with vertical walls; and a convex base drained by perforated bricks. Occasionally, as at Ledston Park and Abbotsford, the icehouse was part of the embankment for a terrace, and its passage linked directly to the house.

When Philip Miller wrote the 1768 edition of *The Gardener's Dictionary*, he set out some key points for the construction of icehouses on country estates: 1) the site must be well drained, or the ice will melt; 2) the site should be open to the sun and wind, not shaded, to prevent dampness; 3) a circular chamber works best; 4) the structure must be well built, able to hold ice for up to three years as insurance against mild winters; 5) the chamber should be sunk into the ground on well-drained sites (such as in sand, gravel or chalk), but raised up in ground that holds moisture.

Sixty years later, in 1829, another commentator recommended that: 1) ice-chamber walls should be built with two skins 18 inches or 2 feet apart, the cavity filled with an absorptive material such as ashes; 2) the top of the chamber should be domed, 'like a soup tureen', with a central hole for loading, linked to a neck with an iron cover that would normally be turfed over; 3) the top of the dome should be covered with a 6-foot thickness of soil and a 'plantation' to give protection from the sun's rays; 4) when removing ice from the chamber, it should first be taken from the sides, using a ladder to descend as the level dropped.

A rediscovered icehouse in Essex has been cleared, revealing the collapse of the brick-vaulted roof to the passage, probably owing to root penetration and the opening up of joints.

Despite the range of helpful publications, as late as 1839 J. C. Loudon observed in his *Encyclopedia* that, in England, many people were still reluctant to build an icehouse because they assumed it had to be cone-shaped and constructed underground, and would be useful only for chilling wine and making ice-cream. He explained that they could be built anywhere and used for preserving meat, fish, fruit and vegetables – 'there is not a more useful appendage to a country house'. Loudon argued that any 'plain square room', if constructed with insulating floors, walls and roof, could preserve ice if it were protected with strong wheat straw or reeds. Doubtless many such chambers survive but are no longer recognised as icehouses.

Some sophisticated icehouses with encircling corridors were built around Edinburgh, perhaps inspired by the agricultural successes of the Scottish Enlightenment. Possibly the earliest is at Dalkeith Palace, built by Henry, 3rd Duke of Buccleuch, on his return from a Grand Tour in 1764. He built on a site above the North Esk River. An unassuming door leads into a passage which changes direction several times before arriving at a huge chamber resembling an up-ended rugby ball, 33 feet 6 inches tall, beautifully formed in stone, with an oculus at the apex. With a diameter of 16 feet, the base of the chamber is fully 23 feet below the floor of the passage, off which six steps lead down into a corridor 5 feet 6 inches wide and 8 feet high, roofed with stone slabs carried on a corbelled cornice.

At Osborne House on the Isle of Wight, Queen Victoria and Prince Albert's summer retreat, the already sophisticated icehouse was refaced in 1853; the vertical walls of its 15-foot-diameter chamber could hold a 14-foot depth of ice. The building was restored in 1995.

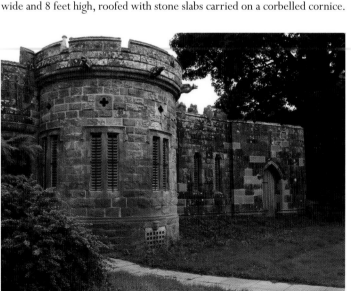

Sir Walter Scott's icehouse (in the right of this picture) at Abbotsford, in the Scottish Borders, was built in 1821, the ornamental game larder in the foreground following over the next few years. Both structures are linked by a tunnel beneath the terrace.

Plans of icehouses drawn to scale to show their comparative sizes. Light blue denotes the widest point of the ice chamber, grey the associated passages and brown the surrounding ground. A is at Mortonhall; B at Dalkeith Palace; and C at Dundas Castle, all near Edinburgh. D is the Cava Arquejada in the hills south of Valencia, Spain; E is at Petworth House, Sussex, below the dairy; F is at Euston Hall, Suffolk, below the Banqueting House; G is at Hampton Court, where the central chamber is surrounded by a further wall, creating voids with no apparent access, except a single passage and on the opposite side a small room with a fireplace; H is at Alva House, Clackmannanshire; and I at High Elms Country Park, Bromley. A family hatchback car is shown at the same scale, for reference.

METRE SCALE

This corridor extends only half way round the chamber, perhaps because of the slope of the ground, possibly because it was experimental or an addition. Later icehouses of this type dispensed with steps and used stone shelves recessed into the walls of the encircling corridor, which went right the way round the main chamber.

At Mortonhall, Edinburgh, the concentric layout probably followed the rebuilding of the house in 1769 or the stables in 1780, but the four openings linking passage and main chamber show the hand of the Royal Engineers in 1939, when the icehouse became an air-raid shelter. The best example is at Dundas Castle, near Edinburgh, where the chamber is 12 feet in diameter, with an oculus for loading, and the encircling corridor, 4 feet wide,

The great chamber at Dalkeith Palace is built from dressed stone that sweeps up into an impressive roof vault, at the centre of which a small circular opening provided ventilation and may have been used for the delivery of crushed ice.

is floored with stone slabs, roofed in vaulted brick and equipped with ten stone shelved recesses 18 inches deep. Loudon's *Encyclopedia* of 1827 commends it as having adjustable apertures for light and air, the shelves ideal for storing freshly cut peas, beans and cauliflower, or retarding potatoes, tubers, bulbs, pot plants and cuttings. Perhaps the primary purpose of such technically advanced structures was horticultural. At a time when great prestige was attached to the introduction of exotic foreign plants, many of these icehouses were located close to walled gardens. Perhaps secretive head gardeners had known for years that keeping seeds cold could increase their chances of germination.

At Dundas Castle, the icehouse door is flanked by openings like windows allowing filtered light and ventilation into the corridor running around the chamber, so that the corridor could be used without disturbing the ice chamber.

OPERATION

BEFORE FILLING an icehouse, it had to be fully dried out, so all doors were opened wide and quicklime might be deployed. Some brick chambers were lined with timber boarding, and most were faced with dry insulating straw before snow or ice was introduced. There was no guarantee it would be available; one Irish icehouse stood empty for three years in the 1740s, awaiting a cold winter.

In the big European chambers, snow was compacted in thin layers separated by straw, so that it could easily be cut out when needed in summer. In later British examples, when snow was used, it was frequently trampled down to form an ice-like mass, and not always layered. It became popular to use crushed ice like a coarse powder, poured through an opening in the crown of the vault; Charles MacIntosh recommended ramming it down inside the chamber, curving the top like a saucer, and adding a little salt water to produce a great mass so firmly compacted it would take a pickaxe to break it. When the level of the entrance passage was reached, the ice would be covered with 6 inches of sawdust or straw, or an old sail cloth or sacking, or even a boarded floor, and a great cold store-room would have been created. After about 1840 blocks of ice began to be imported from abroad, delivered by horse and cart, either stacked in the icehouse or kept in ice chests. Hail was also used: a downfall in the summer of 1758 provided the governor of Williamsburg with ice to cool his wine and freeze cream – some compensation for losing all the windows on the north side of his palace. When the icehouse was filled, it was disturbed as infrequently as possible; the preferred time to visit seems to have been just before sunrise.

If there was no opening in the crown of the vault, and the icehouse had been built with a convoluted passage, filling it would be that much harder. As it was, gathering snow from the fields or collecting ice from a freezing pool must have been exhausting in the shortest days of winter; those working inside the chamber were often half naked, because it became so hot. Five accounts for filling the chamber at Dalkeith survive from 1788–93; between

29 December 1792 and 26 January 1793, thirteen men worked for two days at 10d per man day, using a bushel of salt and consuming twelve dozen rolls and three pints of whisky, costing the Duke of Buccleuch £1 16s 10d. From 1843–53 there were only two years when sufficient ice was available; mild weather, few ponds and the drainage of mines nearby were blamed. Snow was used, and in 1852 the first Norwegian ice arrived, probably brought from Leith docks; the icehouse remained in use until 1914.

On country estates ice came from shallow water features. Sometimes the ice was broken by bouncing an iron chain on it; then men working from a punt would pull fragments to the bank, where it would be broken up finely, collected in sieves and barrowed to the chamber. Flooding the bowling green was another option. At Hanbury Hall, two pools with sluices supplied a shallower freezing pool. The most effective arrangement was when an ice cart could be used to tip directly into the chamber, or a conveyor-belt system could be employed. Commercial icehouses were stocked on a larger scale, by fleets of carts, and later the railway, collecting from places such as the Thames estuary, the Lake District and the Fens. As late as 1896 an 'ice factory' was created on Dartmoor by diverting a stream into artificial trenches.

Between 1569 and 1576 four books describing the uses of snow in the kitchen were published in Seville and Barcelona. In Britain, in the seventeenth century, ice was principally used to chill wine and produce desserts. Making early ice-cream was hard work: ice had to be chipped from the chamber and packed into a vessel with rock salt to form a freezing mixture, placing above it another vessel of cream, milk, sugar and flavouring. Hours of stirring ensued, and the result had to be eaten at once. Yet the principle remained unchanged in 1861, when Mrs Beeton's *Book of Household Management* described pewter freezing pots chilled with a mixture of pounded ice and saltpetre. It is not clear when icehouses began to support a wider menu, but a drawing dated 1719 for 'a royal palace at Kensington' shows an icehouse at the centre of the basement kitchens. When Benedict van Ahlefeldt hosted a summer party in 1736 at his baroque garden in Schleswig-Holstein, guests enjoyed fruit sorbets, iced champagne and marinated fish fillet on crushed ice; his great thatched icehouse survives at Jersbek. Through the eighteenth century, fresh fruits, perfected by the latest technology in the walled garden, would be picked in the morning sun and kept in the icehouse (or dairy), where they

On 5 January 1850 the *Illustrated London News* published a drawing showing how cartloads of ice were collected from the London marshes and taken for sale.

would remain fresh and plump 'for several days'. By 1753 it was observed that in England ice was used for cooling drink less than for fruit and sweetmeats.

From the early nineteenth century it was clear, as the architect John Papworth wrote in 1818, that:

> the icehouse forms an excellent larder for the preservation of every kind of food liable to be injured by heat in summer; thus fish, game, poultry, butter etc. may be kept for a considerable time; indeed in London they are used for such purposes by persons who deal largely in either fish or venison; and for the table, where coolness is desirable, the use of ice in summer is a great luxury.

After about 1840 blocks of imported clear ice became popular in Britain; untouched by straw or salt, they could be displayed ornamentally with butter and jellies, or used as a bed for salads, or added directly to water, milk, wine, spirits, mint juleps, sherry cobblers and ginger beer. On close and sultry days blocks of ice cooled the air. This was fine as long as the ice was clean, but, as population densities increased and ice-harvesting operations intensified, so did the risk of disease from pollution.

Icehouses served ornamental dairies at Petworth, and other large estates as far apart as Kenwood and Taymouth, and they were integrated with other outbuildings too. Picturesque composite towers combining icehouse with game larder were raised at Elvaston, Derbyshire, and Raith Park, Fife, or with a dovecote at Murdostoun, Lanarkshire, and Downhill Demesne, Northern Ireland. At Foxley, near Hereford, a three-storey hexagonal pavilion included all three uses.

At Murdostoun Castle the late-eighteenth-century icehouse occupies the ground floor of an ornamental tower raised on a low mound, to provide an architectural feature, beside the approach to the house. A doocot occupied the upper level.

Game larders are well documented, but the relationship between icehouses and venison in Britain is less understood. At Stanwick St John, a handsome deer shelter stands atop one of three icehouses but any working relationship between them is not known. Deer parks were an important feature of early country estates, and a popular location for icehouses; significantly, venison is most tender if stored for at least a week at around 2 degrees centigrade soon after evisceration. The only known example of a British icehouse specifically used for storing venison was the barrel-vaulted example, now demolished, at Eglinton Castle. Abroad, it was more common: an icehouse '*pour conserver le gibier du roi*' was recorded at Versailles in 1778, and such buildings seem widespread in central Europe. At Betliar, in Slovakia, one barrel-vaulted room was built above another in a north-facing riverside slope, guarded by sphinxes and fed with ice from nearby fishponds.

Since the time of Hippocrates there has been medical use of ice. In Rome, the feverish summer of 1503 claimed the life of the Pope, but his son recovered after immersion 'to the neck' in a big oil jar filled with ice-cold water. Many Mediterranean cities stockpiled ice for the treatment of fever, and in Germany hospitals and mortuary chapels included icehouses. During the Napoleonic Wars Baron Larrey used ice to facilitate battlefield amputations, and in 1850s London, James Arnott combined salt with crushed ice in the treatment of tumours. At Abbotsford, Sir Walter Scott was thankful that ice could be collected one winter's day in 1824, because it treated a friend's fever, while John Ruskin hoped 'to supply invalids in the neighbourhood' from his unsuccessful rock-cut icehouse at Brantwood, Cumbria.

The self-sufficient world of the country estate often included a brewhouse, but none in Britain is known to have used ice. In Bavaria, however, the production of lager after about 1820 required top-cooling, whereby substantial buildings, often with barrel-vaulted roofs, supported an ice store above production facilities, utilising a natural descent of cold air. After about 1870 artificial refrigeration increasingly superseded reliance on diminishing stocks of natural ice. It must have been a huge challenge to maintain large icehouses such as the one built in the 1820s at Calke Abbey. The floor slopes to a central channel, which runs downhill, and the upper chamber could be loaded from the higher end, so perhaps it was filled with ice to cool the lower chamber.

The unusual icehouse at Calke Abbey contains two barrel-vaulted chambers, each 12 feet by 30 feet 6 inches and 12 feet high, with two circular openings in the roof, which, with its earth covering, is 4 feet thick. A loading hatch at the upper end was filled with ice from Dog Kennel Pond.

THE FASHIONABLE ICEHOUSE

W HAT IS NOW Green Park off Piccadilly in London was acquired in the 1660s by the newly crowned Charles II to link Hyde Park to St James's. Charles was inspired by Versailles, and one of his first projects was to put a wall around his new park, plant avenues to delineate The Mall and dig an ornamental canal. It became a favourite place to entertain guests and offer them refreshment. Thus there was an icehouse, 'as the mode is in some parts in France and Italy and other hot Countrys, for to Coole wines and other drinks for the sumer season'.

An icehouse soon became a fashionable accessory in England. At Hampton Court, a 'pretty banqueting house' was set over a cellar in 1662, and in the following year the *Century of Inventions* described 'How to make upon the Thames a floting Garden of pleasure, with Trees, Flowers, Banquetting-Houses, and Fountains, Stews for all kind of fishes, a reserve for Snow to keep Wine in, delicate Bathing places, and the like; with musick…'

Early icehouses complemented geometric parterres, walled gardens, avenues of trees and regular water features – which provided the ice. At Blenheim Palace, Oxfordshire, the great gardens were laid out from 1705, while the palace was being constructed. Maybe the extensive water features included freezing ponds, for by 1707 Henry Wise was completing one of the two icehouses still in existence, mindful of the Duke of Marlborough's comment that 'the most agreeable of all presents is that of ice'.

Layout drawings from the 1720s for the spectacular gardens of Alloa, Clackmannanshire, show icehouses concealed by planting, but more elaborate designs show a delightful icehouse supporting a rotating seat from which to enjoy the view. Four hundred miles south, Charles Bridgeman's 'wilderness' gardens of 1734 at Richmond, Surrey, included canals, a summerhouse and an icehouse with a viewing mount, an arrangement already being enjoyed at the Governor's Palace in Williamsburg, Virginia.

Opposite: Biddulph Grange contains a remarkable collection of themed gardens from the 1840s. This chinoiserie viewing pavilion overlooks a tranquil pool and fronts a small utilitarian icehouse accessible through an artificial tunnel.

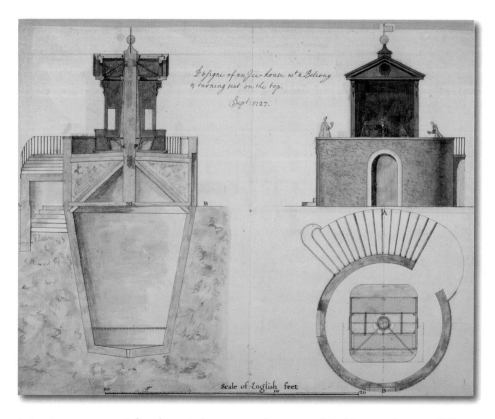

Perhaps keen to demonstrate that an icehouse could be a decorative structure, in 1727 the exiled "Bobbing John" Erskine produced this 'Designe of an Ice-house wt a Belcony & turning seat on the top' for his great garden at Alloa.

Before long, icehouse mounds supported buildings as large as William Kent's banqueting house at Euston (1746), and the principle held good for more than a century, one of the later examples being the Doric viewing seat at Brodsworth Hall. The French loved the idea, as at Gennevilliers (Hauts de Seine, demolished). Such icehouses primarily supplied refreshment, but elsewhere they may have been more closely associated with horticulture; the 1730s town garden at Ayscoughfee, Spalding, still with an icehouse against the perimeter wall, was designed with a canal and statues by an enthusiast for unusual and exotic plants.

The relationship between icehouse and garden pavilion, offering refined hospitality and a little ostentation, reflected architectural fashion. Chinese gardens became increasingly elaborate, popularised by William Chambers, reaching a literal high point in 1762 with the completion of his Great Pagoda at Kew (the nearby icehouse was recorded as in operation by 1763, its contents enjoyed by George III). Many gardens containing Chinese-inspired buildings seem to include icehouses, one of the best examples being the viewing pavilion at Biddulph Grange.

Left: The pleasure gardens of Brodsworth Hall were laid out in the 1860s. The classical covered seat is a great vantage point, at the back of which is the entrance to a modest icehouse underneath, allegedly supplied from a nearby depression that was flooded in winter.

Below: Ayscoughfee Hall in Spalding was built in the fifteenth century, but its 5-acre Dutch-influenced town garden is believed to date from the 1730s. The brick icehouse is screened by topiary against the perimeter wall.

At West Wycombe Park, Buckinghamshire, the 1759 Temple of the Winds, by the second Sir Francis Dashwood, was built above the 'Temple of Winter', and at Stowe, Buckinghamshire, Queen Caroline's Monument by Vanbrugh was in 1764 sited over an existing icehouse. It is not clear whether these icehouses were merely providing a sound foundation or used in conjunction with the new structures above.

There are two notable icehouses at Culzean Castle, probably inspired by Robert Adam's Grand Tour in the 1750s. The more unusual is built into the entrance viaduct spanning the glen. In 1780 it was an architectural innovation, its deliberately 'ruinous' appearance offering a hugely impressive and theatrical arrival to the visitor. To one side was a gazebo, the fireplace still intact: a little building linked by a staircase to a lower suite of rooms including, beneath the viaduct, a 10-foot-diameter egg-shaped icehouse rediscovered by chance in 1982. It seems likely that this icehouse, and possibly others, were supplied from a larger reservoir built at the same time beneath an earth mound closer to Swan Pond, the source of the ice. That icehouse, of rectangular plan, retains an iron eye in its

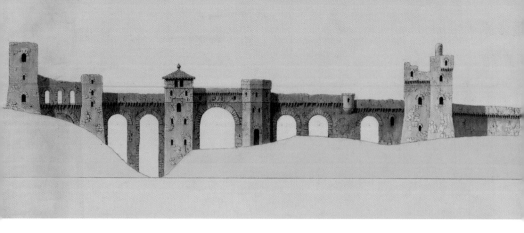

One of Robert Adam's drawings of the 'East Front of the bridge at Culzean Castle' shows a dramatic collection of arches and towers, some 'ruinous', one clearly roofed as some sort of pavilion. Various chambers and a staircase are shown on the plan, but there is no obvious definition of an icehouse.

barrel-vaulted roof, to carry a rope to extract baskets of ice and assist descent into the chamber. If the two icehouses did indeed operate as main reservoir and local outlet, it was not a new idea: when Vignola designed the Villa Giulia in Rome for Pope Julius III in the 1550s, a hillside grotto fronted a large vaulted snow store, from which small loads could be extracted as the need arose. Such an arrangement could explain a relationship between the icehouse at The Drum, Edinburgh, and the nearby subterranean chambers at Gilmerton Cove.

Grottoes and rustic building materials made architectural entrances to icehouses. At Gosford House, the entrance arch mixes honeycombed stone with coloured glass and oyster shells, surmounted by an ornamental finial.

Looking from the ornamental gardens, one would not suspect there was an icehouse within Robert Adam's viaduct at Culzean Castle. It is entered from a vaulted lobby inside the door to the left of the photograph.

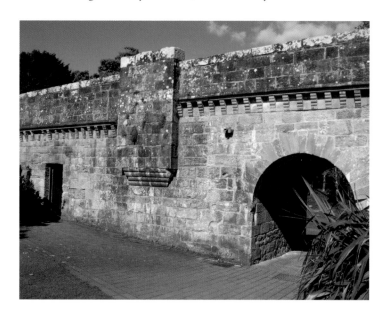

Left: Beneath a grassy mound at the east end of Lily Pond, the Gosford House icehouse near Edinburgh includes stone benches just inside its rustic frontage.

Below: At West Wycombe Park the octagonal Tower of the Four Winds was built, probably after 1755, on top of an icehouse that had been constructed earlier in the century, behind a façade of flint rubble.

The rustic setting and entrance to Ramsdell Hall icehouse, located beside the Macclesfield Canal, on which the ice would probably have been transported.

On a larger scale, Richard Woods's rusticated stone portico at Buckland House, Oxfordshire, is large enough to admit an ice cart. At Forcett Park, North Yorkshire, a dramatic three-bay grotto in dry stonework fronts the long passage to a brick chamber, while at Ramsdell Hall, Cheshire, a key-shaped pool, crossed by a rustic bridge and dotted with a little island, forms the centrepiece to a man-made cascade of rocks which focuses on the pointed-arched icehouse entry, itself surmounted by a primitively carved figure.

From 1770 to 1800 several icehouses were built within pyramids in mainland Europe. Near Paris, at Parc Monceau (1778) and Desert de Retz (1781), they were elements in fantastical evocative landscapes. In 1789 Russian polymath Nikolay Lvov created two splendid examples near Torzhok, and in 1792 another appeared at Potsdam's New Garden, for Frederick William II.

Encouraged by such strongly geometric examples, several notable architects produced icehouse designs in the late eighteenth century, including Nicholas Ledoux at Louveciennes, Yvelines. Some examples were freestanding, whilst others integrated icehouses into service ranges below or beside the main house, as at Cairness, near Fraserburgh, Aberdeenshire, where James Playfair and John Soane drew on the Temple of Vesta in Rome

The pyramidal icehouse at Desert de Retz, restored since 1988, originally illustrated in Georges Le Rouge's *Nouveaux Jardins a la Mode* (Cahier XIII) published in Paris in 1785. He illustrated a similar structure at Stowe (Cahier II), which is likely to have been built, but later demolished.

Vue de la Glaciere.

The New Garden at Potsdam was created from 1787 by Frederick William II of Prussia as a summer residence near his Marble Palace. The designers of the pyramidal icehouse, Carl Gotthard Langhans and Andreas Ludwig Krüger, produced a chamber 17 feet deep, supplied with ice from the Heiliger See. The exterior was decorated with symbols and hieroglyphs.

for inspiration. At the same period in the United States, George Washington built his icehouse at Mount Vernon, Virginia, around 1790. Thomas Jefferson added his in 1803 at Monticello. Perhaps the most spectacular house in America at the time was Hampton Mansion, Maryland; its icehouse, completed around 1800, is 34 feet deep.

Through the nineteenth century improving communications, technology and wealth were reflected in the number of icehouses being built in Britain. In a typical example, the *Morning Post* in May 1805 advertised an elegant villa with stabling for twelve horses, three coach houses, a kitchen garden, pleasure grounds, a verdant lawn and an icehouse. Around 1820 a landscaping project at Cawder House rerouted the river, forming an oxbow lake in the gardens as the setting for a neo-classical-fronted icehouse by David Hamilton. It becomes clear that icehouses served influential buildings; that at Brighton's Royal Pavilion was refurbished for the Prince Regent in 1823.

By this time the icehouses of China were becoming better known in the West. For centuries they had been simple, densely thatched bamboo frames raised on an earth platform. That approach was widely adopted in the United States, and even some more conservative Britons recognised that poles and straw were cheaper and perhaps better-performing than masonry, even if that was not a consideration for the newly rich classes.

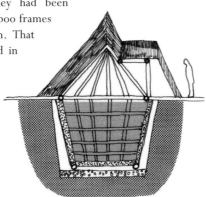

By the 1820s a number of English commentators suggested low-cost icehouses made from timber framing let into a pit and roofed with thatch. This example, from 1825 at Lowther Castle, costing £12 to £15 'answered perfectly' where one costing £250 had failed.

COMMERCIAL ICEHOUSES

THE USE OF ICEHOUSES in early, experimental industrial processes is poorly documented, but it is possible that the large chamber at Warmley, Bristol, 35 feet in diameter and 20 feet high, assisted in the first production of rapidly condensed zinc from English calamine in 1748, when William Champion was developing this important site with its furnaces, mills and grottoes. The brass works was powered from a 13-acre artificial lake and, when it froze, sluices floated lumps of ice towards a hooked conveyor mechanism, to be stored on site or sold to shopkeepers.

Icehouses supporting the fishing industry were built all round Britain, but especially at Berwick-upon-Tweed. Development of the salmon trade led this operation, and probably encouraged the wider use of domestic icehouses for storing foodstuffs. In 1766 boiled and salted salmon was shipped from Berwick, and within twenty years fresh salmon was being sent to London packed in ice, fetching a good price. There was ample demand, for in 1799 7,600 cartloads of ice were brought from local lakes and rivers. The associated storage chambers were cut into Ravesdowne in the 1780s, others at Bankhill following within ten years. These were simple barrel vaults like the nearby military structures, their doorways facing on to the street; some were still in use when the last ice ship arrived from Norway in 1939. But who can say when ice first featured in British fishing? Frampton's *Treatise* of 1580 recalled that Galen (a Roman physician who died around AD 200) 'saieth, that the snowe dooeth cause that the fishe dooeth not corrupt, and so it dooeth conserve it a long time that it rotte not'.

In Scotland, ports such as Helmsdale, Sutherland, had separate icehouses for white fish and salmon. Salmon fishing was an ancient activity, yet few Scottish fishing stations – which combined harbour, bothy, fish house and icehouse – seem to have been built before 1768. In 1787 Cosmo Baron Gordon wrote of the 'adventure' of sending fresh cod and salmon to London and hoped it would be 'advantageous'. It became so – fresh salmon fetched

Opposite:
The brick icehouse at Haven Bridge, Great Yarmouth, was built in 1840 and measures 38 feet by 75 feet internally. It was last loaded in 1899, probably up to windowsill level.

The mouth of an important salmon river was a good location for investment, and a store and boiling house with twin chimneys were already on the Tugnet site in 1783. By 1800 150 people were employed in sending salmon to London, but it is not known exactly when the fish were first sent packed in ice.

twenty times as much as pickled or salted. They were caught late in the summer, so ice to preserve them had to be stored from the previous winter.

Icehouses for the salmon trade were typically stone-built barrel-vaults sheltered under turf, with one chamber to store ice and another to prepare and box the fish, nose to tail, layered in ice. Most examples had an entry door at ground level, allowing direct access to the stored ice, making use of adjacent sloping ground to reach a hatch in the roof, from which ice could be tipped in. After about 1830 there was a marked improvement in nets. One of the biggest and best-known commercial icehouses in Scotland replaced an earlier structure at Tugnet, where the River Spey meets the Moray Firth. It comprises three barrel-vaulted enclosures, about two-thirds of which extended below ground level. Within were six 30-foot-high chambers with cobbled floors equipped with drainage sumps, believed to

have still been operational in 1950. Many other examples survive, particularly on Scotland's east coast, and icehouses for the white fish industry grew too – the *Glasgow Herald* described one 120 by 45 feet, 25 feet high, divided into four chambers – three holding 1,800 tons of ice and one for packing fish. The walls were boarded internally and filled with sawdust. Despite containing 800 tons of ice, the structure was destroyed in a huge fire in 1854.

Herring shoals moved south from Scotland every autumn, the fish reaching prime condition off East Anglia, where a local industry peaked from 1870 to 1914 and Great Yarmouth harbour saw over a thousand boats. Herring that had not been eaten fresh, bloatered, kippered or scotch-cured were 'klondyked' – packed fresh in salt and ice – and mainly exported to Germany. The ice was brought in from frozen broads and rivers to be stored in well-buttressed brick buildings thatched with Norfolk reed. Within a few years, and more often in larger settlements, steam power produced the ice; a tall chimney survives from the Swansea ice factory, which supplied the adjacent fish wharf and enabled trawlers to fish further offshore.

Confectioners built large, functional ice stores, often in the centre of town. As early as 1769, the Edinburgh confectioners Steele & Finch delivered such treats as pineapple ice, and around 1805 John Bridgeman of Marylebone supplied orange, lemon, apricot and raspberry ices, along with meringues and ratafias. William Leftwich joined this trade in London's Fleet Street in 1810, prospering such that after the hot summer of 1821 he took a successful gamble on a consignment of 300 tons of Norwegian ice, enabling him four years later to sink a commercial ice well near Cumberland Market, 82 feet deep and 34 wide, with a capacity of 1,500 tons, stocked from Norway and Greenland.

Commercial ice wells developed under such canny operators as Carlo Gatti, who ran a fleet of ice-delivery carts from 1857 to 1926 and introduced the 'penny ice-cream' to London. He built ice wells along the Regent's Canal and at New Wharf Road, now the London Canal Museum. Gatti also established a continental-style café in Hungerford Market, London, in the 1850s, and icehouses became increasingly associated with commerce and entertainment. Public houses benefited from them. An American example is Gatsby's Tavern; its basement links to an ice well. Several European marketplaces included subterranean icehouses, and English shopping arcades were similarly equipped. The Royal Victoria Arcade, built in Ryde in 1836, included an ice well (with a purveyor of turtle soup above it), along with fourteen retail units, workshops, an art gallery and a wine cellar. All these enterprises and others, including butchers and commercial dairies, needed reliable suppliers of ice, bringing northwards the ancient ice trade.

Carlo Gatti built two ice wells at 12–13 New Wharf Road in King's Cross, London. The first, 34 feet in diameter, was built around 1857; the second, 32 feet in diameter, in 1863. Meltwater was removed by pump. Ice was delivered by barge and subsequently distributed by horse and cart. The depot closed in 1926, but the ice chambers were refurbished in 2013.

Around the Mediterranean the ice trade had been established for centuries. In 1642 Louis XIII issued licences to ice traders in Provence, and by 1770 hundreds of private ice wells were operational in Pistoia, serving Florence until the 1930s. From the 1840s 'ice factories' were built around Berlin, using shallow, sheltered lakes as freezing ponds to supply enormous thatched wooden icehouses. The idea was developed enthusiastically on the east coast of the United States, where the early shipping of ice as ballast from Boston to Havana in 1810 by Frederick Tudor developed into a significant international trade. From 1833 to the 1870s it delivered ice to India, and the plant-collector Joseph Hooker, in Calcutta in 1848, applauded the success of ice in treating inflammation and fever. He also noted the arrival of a box of 391 plants, mostly fruit trees, packed in moss, on an 'ice-ship' from America. When released from cold storage, the buds soon sprouted. For a time Tudor's ships supplied the United Kingdom, but by 1870 most of its ice came from Norway.

ICEHOUSES AROUND THE WORLD

THE SPECTACULAR icehouses of Iran excited English visitors of the 1670s, such as Sir John Chardin, who described the process of filling holes with water and freezing them overnight for collection in the morning. The ice, clear enough to be mixed with water and wine, was stored in pits until summer, then sold by the ass load. Sherbet was best when mixed with snow. Most icehouses were built between 1500 and 1920 on higher ground, serving communities and forts, or refreshing travellers, and taking one of three forms – a dome above a pit, a wall surrounding a roofless pit or an underground vaulted cellar. Domes rising to 65 feet sheltered chambers with internal diameters of 45 feet, the walls tapering in from a 7-foot thickness at the base, built from mud bricks, mortar and plaster, providing insulation from the desert sun, with a vent at the apex. Often the domes were linked to shading walls perhaps 300 feet long, and water management

Meybod icehouse near Yazd, Iran, is 59 feet high with an internal diameter of 59 feet and an external diameter of 75 feet, linking to a shading wall 195 feet long. The icehouse was part of a complete road station, with caravansarai, post relay station, water reservoir and restaurant.

Jaffarabad Jangal icehouse near Tehran has been described as the 'mother of underground icehouses' because of its huge size and a mud-brick shading wall 340 feet long. The building is probably less than a hundred years old; it was served by a deep well.

systems called *qanat* fed the freezing pools that were used when it was impractical to collect snow from the mountains. While some have been restored, many are derelict or have been demolished for redevelopment, and their best documentation has been undertaken by Hemming Jorgensen.

Icehouses in Spain are found on elevated sites from the southern Sierras to the northern Picos, and also on the islands, where the highest peaks have the greatest concentrations. The earliest were built before the reign of Philip II in the mid-sixteenth century, and over the following thirty years, prior to the Armada, visitors from Elizabethan England and from Scotland would have been aware of them in places such as the Escorial, near Madrid. Its encircling walls included stores fed from snowfields in the Guadarrama hills, such as the Royal Snow Pit, 46 feet deep and 28 feet in diameter. This operation led in 1607 to Philip III licensing Pedro Xarquíes to transport snow 50 miles to Madrid to chill soft drinks, thereby creating an organisation that operated until 1863, which regulated the sale of snow from large pits to taverns and private homes. In the snowfields, storage chambers were leased by town halls, monasteries or churches, which levied a tax on snow. The tenant would be responsible for compacting good snow in layers between 8 and 20 inches thick, separated by leaves, ferns or straw, with insulation of bran, rye, brambles, pine needles or even rice hulls. There were celebrations when the chamber was opened in summer, and ice would be wrapped in goatskins and taken on ox-carts to consumers, hospitals and the poor; a pit from 1694 on Gran Canaria supplied snow to an outlet at the back of the cathedral.

The Cava de l'Habitació was built on the Molló del Teix, above Agres in south-eastern Spain, in the early eighteenth century. The chamber is 33 feet deep with an internal diameter of 23 feet, and the site enjoys spectacular views.

In the old town of Bocairente in south-eastern Spain, the Cava de Sant Blai was in use during the eighteenth century, its chamber, 36 feet deep with a 25-foot internal diameter, partially cut out of the living rock. A modern staircase allows visitors to view the interior.

There is an interesting collection of icehouses inland from Alicante, of which the Cava Arquejada is the oldest and best known, reached by a steep track up from the convent at Agres – which replaced an Islamic castle. Its enormous chamber, externally hexagonal, internally circular, is nearly 50 feet in diameter and 40 feet deep, built into rising ground, the lower side being raised into a substantial platform carrying the upper structure. A flared entrance tunnel provides the main access, and six surviving stone ribs describe a crown surmounted by a decorative finial; it operated until 1906. Only a few hundred yards away, looking down over the surrounding plains, is the more typical Cava de l'Habitació, and a little further still is the massively buttressed Cava Don Miguel.

The varied icehouses of Italy deserve better documentation. Among the earliest recorded is the Cortile Ghiacciaia in the Ospedale Maggiore (now the Ca' Granda), which was founded in 1456 to rationalise the hospital facilities of Milan within a huge complex arranged around a series of courts. The icehouse courtyard is believed to date from 1468; following wartime damage and recent restoration, it can now be viewed through a glass roof, and is linked underground to the nearby canal. Out of town, rural icehouses appeared on alpine pastures to cool summer provisions, and on the shores of lakes, such as Varese in Lombardy, they were built by fishermen; the examples at Cazzago Brabbia have been restored since 2000. Two contrasting icehouses are 'twinned' through Valdimagnino Ethnographic Museum in Amagno, where a conical chamber 10 feet wide and 20 high is reached from a room below the Casa del Maestro by a tunnel 40 feet long. Baskets of snow from the winter meadows were used to fill it, and in May the three doors in the passage were sealed up, preserving into summer foodstuffs placed on shelves for the benefit of those who lived above. Its contrasting 'twin' is the early-nineteenth-century icehouse at the Cascina Favaglie Farming Museum in Cornaredo, used until 1945 to preserve butter and cheese in a chamber 33 feet in diameter and 18 feet high, constructed with brick arches, buttresses and chains. In 1771 the *Encyclopedia Britannica* reported that 'the meanest person in Italy who rents a house has a cellar for ice', and many architectural examples survive, such as the moated 'coffee house' on a knoll above the icehouse at the Villa Pisani in the Riviera del Brenta, Venice. It dates back to estate improvements in 1735. The villa was owned by Napoleon and was later a meeting place for Mussolini and Hitler; perhaps they all enjoyed refreshment in '*la casa dei freschi*'.

In France the oldest icehouses are in the south, where some undiscovered Roman examples may survive. As in England, the severe winters of the 1680s, which froze the Grand Canal at Versailles, gave impetus to new construction, though by that time it was already general practice for 'persons of refinement' to drink iced wine. Several sizeable icehouses were built around 1686 at Versailles, with thatched roofs insulating deep wells, and at least one operated until 1909. They were built at the same time that the confectioner Procopio Cuto opened the first café of its type in Paris, selling 'frozen waters' including chilled lemonade and fruit-based *gelato* in porcelain bowls. As in Italy, French icehouses were diverse, ranging from ornamental nineteenth-century examples in Parisian gardens to huge storage chambers constructed in the mountains, as at Pivaut near Mazaugues, now an ice museum. But even they were outclassed by operations at Lac de Sylans, Ain, which grew from 1865 into one of the largest 'ice factories' in Europe, at its peak harvesting 300,000 tons each year and employing three hundred people. The whole lake was used, ice being split into blocks using steam engines, then despatched by rail every summer's day to Paris, Lyon, Marseilles and Algiers, insulated with jute matting, straw and tarpaulins. The site was abandoned in 1925, but monumental ruins survive.

The eighteenth-century markets around Zaragoza in Spain were served by at least twenty-two icehouses. The restored Nevera de la Culroya takes the form of a pit 20 feet deep and of similar diameter, roofed with a characteristic stone vault.

The seventeenth-century icehouse at Brouage, Charente Maritime, was modified in 1707, destroyed in the 1990s, but rebuilt and opened to the public in 2001. The chamber has an internal diameter of 21 feet.

Invitably, there were links between Europe and the New World, exemplified by the fortified towns of Brouage in France and French colonial Quebec, founded in 1608 by Brouage-born Samuel de Champlain, the 'Father of New France'. Both settlements included icehouses within their fortified bastions, built just a few years apart. In Brouage, the Duke of Richelieu's 1688 icehouse served its military hospital. The reason for the icehouse reported in 1692 on one of the corner bastions of Quebec was less clear. Was it for the soldiers' injuries, or to supplement a meagre diet, or because the proposed Château St Louis had to be luxurious enough to receive the king of France if he chose to visit? Evidently it wasn't an innovation; in 1684 the 'good fathers' at the nearby Jesuit college already iced their drinks. Three further forts, two chateaux and additional icehouses followed on the site, which duly fell to the British and is now buried under Dufferin Terrace. A second example, at Detroit, was established under Louis XIV by Antoine Cadillac; in 1701 he built a moated timber stockade. Within

Chateau Vendeuvre in Normandy was completed as a summer retreat in 1752 to designs by Blondel, but the ornamental gardens with water features and ancillary buildings date from 1813. Predictably, the door to this pyramidal icehouse faces north.

four years it included a church, fourteen houses, a powder magazine and an icehouse 15 feet square, extending 15 feet below ground level and 6 feet above, with a lockable door. The British took it over in 1760.

Icehouses flourished in North America, those that graced wealthy estates being modelled on European designs. By far the biggest, with capacities of 40,000 tons or more, were the enormous thatched and timber-framed ice stores supporting the commercial ice trade, insulated with straw and sawdust and built beside freezing lakes, where an acre of foot-thick ice might yield 1,000 tons. The selected area would be cleared of snow, cut with a horse-drawn ice-plough, and broken into blocks to be loaded by steam-powered conveyor into storage, prior to distribution by railway. Today few traces remain. Perhaps the most numerous icehouses, built wherever the climate was suitable, were the small domestic structures perhaps 12 feet square and a similar depth: windowless sheds above a masonry chamber, stocked with ice from a farmer's pond. Thick walls insulated with straw, hay, sawdust or charcoal, externally weather-boarded, supported roofs with overhanging eaves for shade. Sometimes the masonry chamber was omitted, the timber frame extending below ground, providing a cheap if temporary structure that almost anyone could afford.

At the other extreme were the summer residences of the richest families of mainland Europe, where entire households with their retinue of servants would for a few months every year move out of town to rural retreats with elaborate gardens and water features. Thus the Upper Waterworks at Schwetzingen, built from 1762, included a two-storey icehouse complemented by garden pavilions, fountains and a cascade. At Lazienka, near Warsaw, the baroque bath house of 1674 was converted in 1780 into the neoclassical 'Palace on the Water' — summer residence of Poland's last king. When Loudon visited in 1834, he recorded that 'in several places coffee rooms and ice cellars were established and still remain'. Finally, the Austrian Empire of Maria Theresa and Franz Joseph I produced imposing palaces such as Esterhazy and Laxenburg, where large icehouses supported well-stocked hunting grounds within reach of Vienna. There, the spectacular Gloriette of 1775, overlooking the city and Schönbrunn, was built with a vaulted icehouse in the basement, serving the Emperor's breakfast room until it was destroyed in the 1940s.

Replica icehouse, based on an 1866 drawing, built on the estate in Tarrytown, New York, of the American traveller Washington Irving, who stayed for a time at the Alhambra Palace in Spain, where he observed *neveros* gathering snow on the Sierra Nevada.

CONCLUSION

Icehouses began to fall out of use as techniques for artificial refrigeration improved through the later nineteenth century. That coincided with a rise in winter temperatures, so that there was less natural ice to go round at the very time when commercial demand was increasing.

For a time warmer winters stimulated the ice trade. During the 1860s German breweries that relied on local ice to produce lager found their supplies inadequate and had to import it from Scandinavia. In 1870 the huge icehouses of Massachusetts and New York could not be supplied locally, so ice was shipped in from Maine. Icebergs were towed by boat. Enormous quantities of Norwegian ice were delivered to ports all around the United Kingdom, peaking in about 1899 then declining until the watershed of the First World War, leaving minimal trade through to the 1930s. New steam-powered machines manufactured ice for distribution by horse and cart to householders, who would store it in 'portable icehouses' or 'refrigerators' made of well-seasoned wood, lined with zinc. Those who remembered Thomas Masters' pioneering 'elegant and portable' domestic icebox, first described in 1844, would have agreed with his prediction: 'When we consider how the cumbrous machinery of the ice well is here superseded by an elegant and portable machine, so simple in construction that it can be put into operation even by a child, the progress of improvement may indeed be described as having reached its climax.'

As country estates declined after the First World War, domestic icehouses increasingly fell into disuse and were abandoned, except in more remote locations where mains electricity was still absent in the 1950s.

Mehdiabad icehouse in Markazi province, Iran, about 30 miles north of the town of Saveh, takes the form of a stepped cone, 33 feet in internal diameter at the base, with a vent at the apex. It is from the Qadjar period (1780s to 1925) and has been well restored.

An icehouse, probably for the salmon trade, was built c. 1833 at Duntrune Castle, at the mouth of the Crinan Canal, which provided shipping with a short cut from Glasgow to the Western Isles. It was converted in 2012 to a small dwelling.

In 1980 an 'Ice House Hunt' in the United Kingdom stimulated a revival of interest in these structures, since when many have been rediscovered, documented and refurbished. Unfortunately, a few chambers have been filled with earth in the name of safety, when an openwork grating would have been sufficient to prevent unwary visitors from falling in, as well as providing ventilation and the opportunity for inspection. Where chambers are accessible, they offer a unique atmosphere and eerie acoustic qualities. Many icehouses are still in a state of benign neglect, retaining their mystery and sometimes sheltering bats, threatened only by tree roots and open joints. Growing numbers, all over the world, can be visited in country parks and the grounds of historic houses, where they assist the understanding of gardens, food, social status, commercial enterprise and climate change. A few have been converted into small galleries; others have been equipped with solar-powered lighting. Some commercial icehouses have reopened as displays within museums, and a few have become tiny dwellings. Strangely, increasing energy costs and a few degrees of climate change could conceivably return them to their original use.

Ballina Hotel in County Mayo, Ireland, is a converted salmon fishery, built in 1836 on the Moy estuary. At its height, it exported forty thousand salmon to Scotland annually, as well as to Dublin and Liverpool. The ice chamber is now a restaurant.

FURTHER READING

Beaudet, Pierre R. *Under the Boardwalk in Quebec City: Archaeology in the Courtyard and Gardens of the Chateau Saint-Louis.* Guernica Editions Inc, 1990.

Carson, Charles J. T. *Technology and the Big House in Ireland: c.1800 – c. 1930.* Cambria Press, 2009.

David, Elizabeth. *Harvest of the Cold Months: the Social History of Ice and Ices.* Faber & Faber, 2011.

Fagan, Brian M. *The Little Ice Age: How Climate Made History 1300–1850.* Basic Books, 2002.

Jorgensen, Hemming. *Ice Houses of Iran.* Mazda Publishers, Costa Mesa, USA, 2012.

Weightman, Gavin. *The Frozen Water Trade – How Ice from New England Lakes Kept the World Cool.* Harper Collins Publishers, 2003.

PLACES TO VISIT

This is a list of the locations of icehouses that can be seen by the public. National Trust properties in England, Wales and Northern Ireland are indicated by the letters 'NT'; in Scotland by 'NTS'; English Heritage 'EH' and Historic Scotland 'HS'

UNITED KINGDOM

ENGLAND

Ashton Court, Long Ashton, Bristol BS41 9JN. Telephone: 0117 963 3438.

Attingham Park, Atcham, Shrewsbury, Shropshire SY4 4TP. Telephone: 01743 708162. (NT)

Avoncroft Museum of Historic Buildings, Stoke Heath, Bromsgrove, Worcestershire B60 4JR. Telephone: 01527 831363.

Ayscoughfee Hall Museum and Gardens, Church Gate, Spalding, Lincolnshire PE11 2RA. Telephone: 01775 764555.

Berwick on Tweed, examples at Bankhill and Shoregate.

Biddulph Grange Garden, Grange Road, Biddulph, Staffordshire ST8 7SD. Telephone: 01782 517999. (NT)

Brantwood, Coniston, Cumbria LA21 8AD. Telephone: 015394 41396.

Brodsworth Hall and Gardens, Brodsworth, Doncaster, South Yorkshire DN5 7XJ. Telephone: 01302 724969. (EH)

Burton Manor, The Village, Burton, Neston, Cheshire CH64 5SJ. Telephone: 0151 336 5172.

Calke Abbey, Ticknall, Derby DE73 7LE. Telephone: 01332 863822. (NT)

Charborough Park, Wareham, Dorset BH20 7EW.
  Telephone: 01258 857204.
Chilston Park, Lenham, Kent ME17 2BE. Telephone: 0845 072 7426
Christchurch Park, Bolton Lane, Ipswich, Suffolk IP4 2BX.
  Telephone: 01473 252435.
Cirencester Park, Coates, Cirencester, Gloucestershire GL7 6LA.
  Telephone: 01285 640410.
Compton Verney, near Stratford-upon-Avon, Warwickshire CV35 9HZ.
  Telephone: 01926 645500.
Croome, near High Green, Worcester WR8 9DW.
  Telephone: 01905 371006. (NT)
Duncombe Park, Helmsley, North Yorkshire YO62 5EB.
  Telephone: 01439 770213.
Farnborough Hall, Farnborough, near Banbury, Oxfordshire OX17 1DU.
  Telephone: 01295 690002. (NT)
Great Yarmouth: Bridge Road, Great Yarmouth, Norfolk NR31 0QS.
Greys Court, Rotherfield Greys, Henley-on-Thames, Oxfordshire RG9 4PG.
  Telephone: 01491 628529. (NT)
Haggerston Castle, Beal, Berwick-upon-Tweed, Northumberland TD15 2PA.
Hampton Court Palace, East Molesey, Surrey KT8 9AU.
  Telephone: 0844 482 7777.
Hanbury Hall, School Road, Hanbury, Droitwich, Worcestershire
  WR9 7EA. Telephone: 01527 821214. (NT)
Hatchford Park, Ockham Lane, Cobham, Surrey KT11 1LR.
Hatchlands Park, East Clandon, Guildford, Surrey GU4 7RT.
  Telephone: 01483 222482.
Heveningham Hall, Heveningham, Suffolk IP19 0PN.
High Elms Country Park, Shire Lane, Farnborough, Orpington, Kent
  BR6 7JH.
Holkham Hall, Holkham, Wells-next-the-Sea, Norfolk NR23 1AB.
  Telephone: 01328 710227.
Holland Park, Ilchester Place, Kensington, London W8 6LU.
  Telephone: 020 7602 2226.
Hoveton Hall, Hoveton, Norwich, Norfolk NR12 8RJ.
  Telephone: 01603 782798.
Kedleston Hall, near Quarndon, Derby DE22 5JH.
  Telephone: 01332 842191. (NT)
Kentwell Hall, Long Melford, Suffolk CO10 9BA.
  Telephone: 01787 310207.
Kenwood House, Hampstead Lane, Hampstead, London NW3 7JR.
  Telephone: 0870 333 1181. (EH)
Knole, Sevenoaks, Kent TN15 0RP. Telephone: 01732 462100. (NT)

Levens Hall, Kendal, Cumbria LA8 0PD. Telephone: 01539 560321.

London Canal Museum, 12–13 New Wharf Road, London N1 9RT.
Telephone: 020 7713 0836.

Ludlow Castle, Castle Square, Ludlow, Shropshire SY8 1AY.
Telephone: 01584 874465.

Lydiard Park, Lydiard Tregoze, Swindon, Wiltshire SN5 3PA.
Telephone: 01793 466664.

Moseley Park, Moseley, Birmingham B13 8DD.

Mottingham, The Tarn, Court Road, Mottingham, London SE9 5QE.

Mottisfont, near Romsey, Hampshire SO51 0LP.
Telephone: 01794 340757. (NT)

Mount Edgcumbe House and Country Park, Cremyll, Torpoint, Cornwall PL10
1HZ. Telephone: 01752 822236.

Nottingham: City of Caves, Drury Walk, Upper Level, Broadmarsh Shopping
Centre, Nottingham NG1 7LS. Telephone: 0115 988 1955.

Osborne House, York Avenue, East Cowes, Isle of Wight PO32 6JX.
Telephone: 01983 200022.

Osterley Park and House, Jersey Road, Isleworth, Middlesex TW7 4RB.
Telephone: 020 8232 5050. (NT)

Painshill, Portsmouth Road, Cobham, Surrey KT11 1JE.
Telephone: 01932 868113.

Petworth House and Park, Petworth, West Sussex GU28 0AE.
Telephone: 01798 342207. (NT)

Prior Park Landscape Garden, Ralph Allen Drive, Bath, Somerset BA2 5AH.
Telephone: 01225 833422. (NT)

Royal Botanic Gardens, Kew, Richmond, Surrey TW9 3AB.
Telephone: 020 8332 5655.

Royal Victoria Arcade, Union Street, Ryde, Isle of Wight PO33 2LQ.

Rufford Abbey, Ollerton, Nottinghamshire NG22 9DF.
Telephone: 0870 333 1181. (EH)

Scotney Castle, Lamberhurst, Tunbridge Wells, Kent TN3 4QR.
Telephone: 01892 893820. (NT)

Seaton Delaval Hall, The Avenue, Seaton Sluice, Northumberland
NE26 4QR. Telephone: 0191 237 9100. (NT)

Shugborough Estate, Milford, near Stafford ST17 0XB.
Telephone: 0845 459 8900. (NT)

Stourhead, near Mere, Wiltshire BA12 6QD.
Telephone: 01747 841152. (NT)

Studley Royal Deer Park, Fountains, Ripon, North Yorkshire HG4 3DY.
Telephone: 01765 608888. (NT)

Syon House, Syon Park, London Road, Brentford, Middlesex TW8 8JF.
Telephone: 020 8758 1888.

Tyntesfield, Wraxall, Bristol BS48 1NX. Telephone: 01275 461900. (NT)

Wallington, Cambo, near Morpeth, Northumberland NE61 4AR.
    Telephone: 01670 773600. (NT)

Warmley, Bristol Kingswood Heritage Museum, Tower Lane, Bristol.
    Telephone: 0117 960 5664.

Weeting Castle, Weeting, Norfolk IP27 0AQ. Telephone: 0870 333 1181. (EH)

West Wycombe Park, West Wycombe, HP14 3AJ. Telephone: 01494 513569.
    (NT)

Wrest Park, Silsoe, Bedfordshire MK45 4HR. Telephone: 01462 674671. (EH)

Wycombe North Riding, YO13 9QA (near All Saints Church).

York: Monk Bar Icehouse, York.

NORTHERN IRELAND

Carnfunnock Country Park, Larne, Country Antrim.
    Telephone: 0208 2827 0541.

Castle Coole, Enniskillen, County Fermanagh BT74 6JY.
    Telephone: 028 6632 2690. (NT)

Downhill Demesne, Mussenden Road, Castlerock, County Londonderry
    BT51 4RP. Telephone: 028 7084 8728. (NT)

Loughgall Country Park, Main Street, Loughgall, County Armagh BT61
    8HZ. Telephone: 028 3889 2900.

SCOTLAND

Applecross Estate (the Applecross Trust), Applecross, Highland IV54 8ND.
    Telephone: 01520 744482.

Bettyhill, former fishing station, Scrabster, Sutherland KW14 7SX.

Culzean Castle, Maybole, Ayrshire KA19 8LE. Telephone: 01655 884400.
    (NTS)

Dalkeith Country Estate, Dalkeith, Midlothian EH22 2NJ.
    Telephone: 0131 654 1666.

Duff House, Banff AB45 3SX. Telephone: 01261 818181. (HS)

Eglinton Country Park, Irvine, North Ayrshire KA12 8TA.
    Telephone: 01294 551776.

Findhorn: Village Icehouse and Heritage Centre, Findhorn, Forres, Moray
    IV36 3YE.

Glamis Castle, Dundee Road, Glamis, Angus DD8 1RJ.
    Telephone: 01307 840393.

Gosford House, Longniddry, East Lothian EH32 0PY.
    Telephone: 01875 870808.

Hermitage of Braid, Braid Road, Edinburgh EH10 6JF.

Hopeman: Harbour Street, Hopeman, Moray.

Kelburn Castle, Fairlie, Ayrshire KA29 OBE. Telephone: 01475 568685.

Paxton House, near Berwick-upon-Tweed TD15 1SZ.
  Telephone: 01289 386291.
Penicuik House, Penicuik, Midlothian EH26 9LA.
St Andrews Castle, The Scores, St Andrews, Fife KY16 9AR.
  Telephone: 01334 477196. (HS)
Tentsmuir Point, Tentsmuir National Nature Reserve and Forest KY16 0DR
  (Forestry Commission Scotland).
Tugnet Icehouse, Scottish Dolphin Centre, Tugnet, Spey Bay, Fochabers,
  Moray IV32 7DU. Telephone: 01249 449500.

WALES

Dinefwr, Llandeilo, Carmarthenshire SA19 6RT. Telephone: 01558 824512.
  (NT)
Dunraven Park, St Bride's Major, Vale of Glamorgan CF32 0TF.
Hafod Estate, Pontrhydygroes, Ystrad-Meurig, Ceredigion SY25 6DX.
National Botanic Garden of Wales, Llanarthne, Carmarthenshire SA32 8HG.
  Telephone: 01558 667149.
Penrhyn Castle, Bangor, Gwynedd LL57 4HN. Telephone: 01248 353084. (NT)
Pontypool Museum, St David's Close, Pontypool, Torfaen NP4 6JH.
  Telephone: 01495 762200.
Powis Castle and Garden, Welshpool, Powys SY21 8RF.
  Telephone: 01938 551944. (NT)
Tredegar House, Newport NP10 8YW. Telephone: 01633 815880. (NT)

FRANCE
Chateau de Vendeuvre, Vendeuvre 14170, Normandy.
Desert de Retz, Allee Frederic Passy, 78240 Chambourcy, Île-de-France.
La Musee de la Glace & Glaciere Pivaut, Hameau du Chateau, 83136
  Mazaugues, Var, Provence-Alpes-Cote d'Azur.
Petit Trianon (near Lac de Trefle), Palace de Versailles, Place d'Armes,
  Versailles, Paris 78000.
Richelieu's Bastion, Brouage, Charente Maritime.

GERMANY
Beuing Brothers former Brewery, Altenberge, North Rhine-Westphalia.
Bliesdalheim (off Bliestalfreizeitweg) Saarland.
New Garden, 14467 Potsdam, Brandenburg.
Schloss Schwetzingen, 68723 Schwetzingen, Baden-Wurttemberg.
Schloss Wustrau, 16818 Wustrau-Altfriesach, Brandenburg.

IRELAND
Belvedere House, Mullingar, County Westmeath.

Blarney Castle, Blarney, County Cork.
Dun Na Ri Forest Park, Kingscourt, County Cavan.
Dunsandle Castle, Kiltullagh, Athenry, County Galway.
Grange Loop Walk near ruins of Kilcooly Abbey, South Tipperaray.

ITALY

Ca' Granda (Ospedale Maggiore), Via Festa del Pardano 7, 20122, Milan.
Cazzago Brabbia icehouses, shoreline of Lake Varese, Lombardy.
Cascina Favaglie Rocco, Via Merendi 28, 20010 Cornaredo, Milan.
Ghiaccio della Madonnina, Ecomuseo della Montagna Pistoiese, Pistoia, Le Piastre SR66, Pistoiese-Modenese.
Villa Pisani, Via Doge Pisani 7, 30039 Stra, Venice.

SPAIN

La Cava Arquejada, Montcabrer (Route 027-10), Agres, Alcoi, North Alicante.
Cava de Sant Blai, Bocairent, Vall d'Albaida, Valencia.
Pozo de Hielo de la Barbacana, Calle Pozo de Hielo, Barrio de St Juan, 22300 Barbastro, Huesca.
Nevera de la Culroya, Fuendetodos 50142, Zaragoza.
Palacio de los Reyes de Navarra de Olite, Plaza Carlos III El Noble, Navarre.

UNITED STATES OF AMERICA AND CANADA

Cape Pond Ice, 104 Commercial Street, Fort Point Wharf, Gloucester, Maryland 01930.
Fort William Historical Park, King Road, Thunders Bay, Ontario P7K 1L7.
Gatsby's Tavern Museum, 134 North Royal Street, Alexandria, Virginia 22314.
Georgian Museum, 105 East Wheeling Street, Lancaster, Ohio 43130.
Governor's Palace, Williamsburg, Virginia 23187.
Hampton Historic Site, 535 Hampton Lane, Towson, Maryland 21286.
Hancock Shaker Village, Lebanon Mountain Road, Hancock, Maryland 01237.
Ice House Museum, Sturgis Park, Cedar Falls, Iowa 50613.
McClean Ice House, Appomatox Court House Historic Park, Virginia 24522.
Monticello, 931 Thomas Jefferson Parkway, Charlottesville, Virginia 22902.
Tallgrass Prairie National Preserve, Strong City, Kansas 66869.

INDEX